SKIING THE ROCKIES

SKIING THE ROCKIES

PHOTOGRAPHY BY BRUCE BARTHEL

TEXT BY CHARLIE MEYERS

GRAPHIC ARTS CENTER PUBLISHING COMPANY
PORTLAND, OREGON

International Standard Book Number 0-912856-60-2
Library of Congress Catalog Card Number 80-65133
Copyright© 1980 by Graphic Arts Center Publishing Co.
P.O. Box 10306 • Portland, Oregon 97210 • 503/224-7777
Designer • Robert Reynolds
Typesetting • Paul O. Giesey/Adcrafters
Printer • Graphic Arts Center
Bindery • Lincoln & Allen
Printed in the United States of America
Second Printing

Steamboat calls its snow "champagne powder," which seems as good a description as any for the ultimate conditions on the Shadows run, typical of the fine tree skiing on one of Colorado's most popular mountains.

Title page: Moguls, those hummocks of snow created by the successive carving action of skis on a steep slope, are the bane of the learning skier, the joie de vivre of the expert. Few are more imposing than on Holiday Run at Sun Valley.

The exhilarating sense of openness comes with skiing at Snowmass. Left: World Freestyle Champion Scott Brooksbank executes a reverse somersault with full twist. Overleaf: An approaching storm spurs skiers across the ridge of Siberia Bowl at Vail.

Speed, the single essential ingredient of ski racing, translates into posture, concentration and even the helmet design of a professional racer in a downhill event at Aspen.

Skiing the trees. Timber bashing. By any name, many consider it the most satisfying of ski experiences when evergreen glades hang heavy with new snow from an overnight storm.

The ambience of après ski shines through the window of a popular
Victorian-style restaurant at Crested Butte, Colorado. Fine restaurants and
night spots are an additional reason tourists select Rocky Mountain resorts.

The precipitous pitch of Al's Run at Taos has intimidated more than one arriving skier, prompting management to erect a sign in the parking lot reassuring visitors that this run is only a small portion of the total area.

Mushroom Cliffs is a vividly descriptive name given to these exotic creations of snow, rock and wind at Arapahoe Basin, Colorado.

*Backlighting on a solid blanket of flying snow crystals seems to propel
a skier into his own shadow at Snow Basin, Utah.*

Cross-country skiing, once almost exclusively an activity of the East and Midwest, rapidly is gaining popularity in the Rockies. A solitary skier skirts an aspen grove at Jackson Hole, Wyo.

16

DIGGING FOR ROOTS

I am sitting in the middle of a makeshift camp: a light mountain tent, a couple of snowcaves and a sputtering portable stove upon which perches, precariously, I fear, a mulligan stew which will serve the dual purpose of warmth and nourishment.

A light snow is swirling gently on a growing wind sweeping down off the flanks of barren peaks to the north and west. With the approach of darkness, the scene is ominous, Wagnerian. The wind's presence is chronicled in the flickering of the stove and a low moaning in the scrub evergreens clinging to a tenuous existence so close to timberline.

Bundled in a goose-down parka with my feet snugged into down booties, I am warm enough for the moment, but the anticipation of impending sleep atop ten feet of snow holds little appeal. Thoughts of the morrow are a mixture of emotions: another day of skiing under heavy pack; more climbing, almost straight uphill, to a craggy, windblown summit where the view will thrill the senses; elation at having made it there; then a long, plummeting descent which will tax endurance, ability and control I have not yet fully achieved.

Fully eight hours ago we had begun this ski touring adventure with high spirits which caused us to float, skis scarcely touching the ground, over delicate snowbridges. We laughed our way over vast snowfields and snapped pictures of pine squirrels and Canada jays and wondered at the many animal tracks which crisscrossed our path.

But now my thoughts turned more to the comforts of Crested Butte, where our journey began, where there would be the warmth of a roaring fire, soothing beverages, music, pretty girls. Crested Butte, that old mining town reincarnated as a bright new ski resort, is the kind which seems to sprout like mushrooms after a spring rain. Only now the nourishment is snow and tourists.

Owing in equal parts to its location in south central Colorado and an effective marketing thrust, Crested Butte has become something of an extension of the New South, where people bring their drawls and you-alls to experience the hottest bit of action since William Tecumseh Sherman's big barbecue on Peachtree Boulevard. In fact, there is a bit of logic rampant among mountain folk which holds that the inspiration for this southern exodus to the slopes is revenge, pure and simple.

About the same distance in the opposite direction—through a narrow notch of a pass in an imposing granite wall, then down a steep, avalanche-strewn slit of a valley—lies our destination, Aspen.

The name has become household: so chic, so sleek, so much a part of noveau Americana that they name automobiles and soft drinks for it. It is the same Aspen to which the networks regularly dispatch full camera crews all the way from New York just to test the wind and maybe check for a pulse. Or perhaps raise their own.

Aspen is another old mining town which caught the ski bug almost a quarter century before Crested Butte. It has spent the last couple of decades serving as the bad example—one which Crested Butte folks say they should not follow. Ah, success. Like beauty, it is so much in the eye of the beholder.

Back to my point equal distant to this teapot tempest, back to the reality of this potentially hostile place to which I somehow have transported myself by dint of stub-

bornness and some minor talent. The snow is swirling harder now, and, one by one, we mumble good-nights and drift off to our chosen warrens for sleep.

I lie on my back taking sparse comfort from a urethane pad which, considering the state of the petroleum business, soon may be a collector's item and listen to the soft hiss of corn snow on nylon. The sensation of being very alone, of reliance on my own devices and a slender, willowy pair of skis, returns stronger than ever.

Suddenly it hits me, something I had been reading about just a few days before. *This is what it was like for Father John Dyer. This is how he did it a hundred years ago.* For Rocky Mountain skiing, the circle again is complete. Or, for a few hardy souls who kept the faith, perhaps it never was broken. Such is the appeal of skiing, a sport which can be several things to all people—from the wilderness experience far from anyone or anything to the disco cacophony and manicured trails of Aspen and Vail.

Nowhere does each of these come together with more impact and appeal than in that distinctive jumble of snow-clad peaks which reach from Alaska to Mexico and beyond, mountains which were folded in Cretaceous time yet are more a part of the future than the past.

This is the Rocky Mountains. This is skiing.

GENESIS

Even in another time and place the figure teetering on a barren snowfield high above some remote mining camp must have appeared laughable: bulky greatcoat, outsized fur hat, long skis — particularly the skis. They were upturned wooden appendages fully twelve feet long which ensured that the descent to the town below would be difficult and graceless at best.

This was skiing in the Rocky Mountains just after the Civil War, a time when men from the East and South, some trying to remember and others to forget, poured into the high country in search of precious metals. A few of those from the upper Midwest knew how to ski, and a few others would try to learn. From this beginning and the mounting enthusiasm of the many who came after them, skiing has evolved into an enterprise whose related investments are measured in the billions of dollars. It has taken a while and, often, it hasn't been easy.

Despite the prevailing notion that nothing really has existed until the mass media discovers it, skiing has been with us for a long time. Carbon dating of wood remnants, unmistakably skis, from prehistoric northern Europe places their age at 4,500 years.

These skis, which early cave drawings showed to be more than ten feet long, were born of necessity, of the need to travel quickly and to pursue game in a region covered by snow much of the year. Later, skis had profound military utility, a swift-strike capacity which brought armed men down upon an unsuspecting foe in the dead of winter. The skis bear a marked resemblance to those used today, a fact which might give modern ski designers pause to reflect on what they've been doing all this time.

War games perhaps spawned the first competition, and at some juncture it occurred to these hardy Norsemen that skiing was just plain fun. Clearly, Scandinavia was the cradle from which the skiing gospel was so lovingly and enthusiastically spread to the rest of the world.

Reflecting the necessities of its origin, Scandinavian skiing remained a practical undertaking. There was cross-country, hardly more than an extension of the need to travel. For macho and bravado, fulfilling the primal need to compete, ski jumping was manhood's proving ground. Although many Scandinavians now indulge in downhill skiing, little has changed for most of them.

It wasn't until the latter years of the 19th century that Central Europe got into the swing of things. Here, the environmental influence of steep mountains thrust skiing into yet another direction; schussing down these precipitous slopes demanded turning to control speed and shorter skis for maneuverability.

Although the two regions are separated by only a few hundred miles and there was much interaction between the two, the dichotomy between Nordic and Alpine skiing deepened with the years. Only in recent times have skiers felt free to cross the line of demarcation and participate enthusiastically in both.

Surprisingly, it was fervent Scandinavian immigrants who first brought their form of skiing to the New World. Moving first into the upper Midwest and then on to the gold camps of the Rockies and Sierra, they soon were imitated by miners and ranchers hungry for some sport to pass the long winters. Most mountain valleys bore the tracks of these "Norwegian snowshoes."

But it was the johnny-come-lately alpinists who were to have the most lasting influence. The greater ease and excitement of downhill skiing proved far more in keeping with the galloping American social trends in the middle years of this century. Only recently has the trend reversed, and have quantities of American skiers, perhaps as an extension of the jogging craze, become enamored of running cross-country over snow.

Although there must have been some doughty old Norwegian as catalyst, the earliest record of skiing in the Rockies was manifested in the rather dramatic personality of Father John Lewis Dyer, a Methodist minister who arrived from Ohio in 1861.

Father Dyer's mission was a rollicking camp with the intriguing name of Buckskin Joe near the Colorado town of Breckenridge. His ministry was almost as vast as the mountains themselves, and there is evidence that in the true spirit of the circuit rider he journeyed as far south as New Mexico to care for a diverse and often unruly flock.

In the winter of 1862 Dyer began using skis on his missions, frequently crossing the Continental Divide or negotiating the uncommonly hazardous route over 13,186-foot Mosquito Pass, highest in all the Rockies. In addition to his chosen work of spreading the gospel, Father Dyer was given a government contract to carry the mail. Laden with a fifty-pound pack, he somehow managed to make his way over steep pitches and deep-drifted snows on journeys of thirty-five miles or more.

Shortly thereafter, yet another skiing minister, Rev. George Darley, made his rounds through the rugged San Juan Mountains of southwestern Colorado. Following these examples, miners and mailmen routinely used the long, wooden skis for winter transportation. Reflecting the Scandinavian-born desire to race, the first recorded Rocky Mountain competition, a downhill, was contested near Crested Butte in 1886.

Further north, Norwegian immigrants drifting westward out of Minnesota and the Dakotas brought their "snowshoes" into Montana. Through much the same progression, these long skis were introduced to mining camps in Utah,

Wyoming, and New Mexico—many of which would, for quite different reasons, evolve as major ski resorts almost a century later.

Far up in these lofty, snowy, and generally isolated realms, skiing continued to gain acceptance through the years. Early skiing, affixed these long, curved skis to the feet with tenuous leather thongs, was of a singular form and mind. It consisted almost exclusively of a long, tiring climb up snowfields followed by a straight, death-defying schuss to the bottom. As one vintage daredevil described it, "Sure you could turn on those old skis. You could turn almost all the way around. But the skis wouldn't."

Imagine the spectacle of a heavily bundled skier trying to keep his balance with nothing more than a pole used somewhat like a rudder for stability. Skiing then was a very long way from stretch pants and buckle boots and cracked metal edges.

When the boom went bust in all the mining towns, it remained for a scattering of Johnny Appleseeds, almost exclusively of Nordic origins, to keep the flame alive through the difficult years of World War I and pave the way for the true awakening of the sport in the 1930s.

One such man was Karl Hovelsen, anglicized to Carl Howelsen, who came first to Denver, then Hot Sulphur Springs and, finally, to the sleepy little Colorado ranching town of Steamboat Springs in 1913. Here, in a free-spirited community, he found that special ingredient of enthusiasm for which he had searched the continent.

Steamboaters took to running and jumping on skis with a fervor which amazed even Howelsen, an enthusiasm which produced an unbroken succession of Olympic skiers. For decades, it seemed as if the United States Ski Team might be composed almost exclusively of residents of this small cow town of a few hundred people.

In Utah, a band of hearty Norwegians converted to the Mormon faith were doing what came naturally. They built a ski jump in 1916 and not long after lured the Engen boys—Alf, Sverre and Corey. The Wasatch mountains soon rang with the heavily accented shouts of these modern Norsemen. Yet when economic conditions mellowed to accommodate skiing's first real growth spurt later in the 1930's, it was Alpine skiing, that dashing, glamorous import from central Europe, which caught the fancy of those adventuresome enough to try.

For the most part, skiing became a society venture propagated by industry moguls. Walter Paepcke, president of the Container Corporation of America, became the driving force behind Aspen and farther north, Averell Harriman, board chairman of Union Pacific Railroad, sent an Austrian count to locate a ski resort which would serve the dual purpose unheard of in the history of either railroading or skiing. What Count Felix Schaffgotsch settled on, Sun Valley, Idaho, became both the world's first resort built exclusively for winter sports and a dazzling inducement for people to ride Harriman's railroad to get there. Back in the post-depression days a million dollars was a lot of money, and Harriman was thought quite mad for spending three to acquire 4,300 acres and build the facilities which would make Sun Valley the unchallenged showpiece of the sport for years to come. Harriman shuttled a steady stream of stars from a burgeoning Hollywood movie industry to his resort, further giving skiing the reputation of an activity of the affluent.

And so it was, save for a few hardy individuals clinging

18

to their mountain enclaves. Society groups in Denver began making weekend junkets to the deep-snow country around Loveland and Berthoud passes and to a secluded glen at the far side of a railroad tunnel through the Continental Divide which later would be known as Winter Park. In Salt Lake City, their counterparts needed an even shorter journey to frolic on the steep slopes of the Wasatch.

A major breakthrough was achieved with the advent of lifts. At first they were rudimentary rope tows powered by automobile engines. But chairlifts came soon after, and it no longer was necessary to make long, exhausting climbs to enjoy skiing. But to most Americans, skiing remained an outlandishly absurd undertaking, something akin to jumping out of an airplane without a parachute. It wasn't until after World War II, when the nation throbbed to a new spirit of adventure and mobility, that skiing began truly to take wing.

In many ways the Great War was a godsend to American skiing in general and to the Rocky Mountains in particular. Expert skiers from Austria and Switzerland fleeing the march of Adolph Hitler and the ravages of war migrated in some numbers to New England and then points west, where they became the impetus for a dramatic ski growth in the years immediately preceding America's entry into the conflict. These hardy easterners then became the core of the famed Tenth Mountain Division, America's ski troops, who trained high in the central Colorado Rockies at a place called Camp Hale.

With vivid recollections of the majestic mountains and the depth and quality of the snow, these same men flocked back to the Rockies soon after the war to give impetus to the second great economic boom to hit these mountains, this one based on the more and plentiful reliable standard of white gold. Easterners like Steve Bradley, a former Dartmouth College racer, came to thrust Winter Park into the midst of this renaissance, while Pete Seibert selected a sheep pasture not far from the site of his mountain troop training and founded a place in 1962 he called Vail.

When the 1960 Winter Olympics came to Squaw Valley, California, further whetting the nation's growing ski appetite, more than half of the ski officials were imported from Colorado. The Rockies now had the mountains, the ideal snow, and the knowledge to make it all work. The second rush was on.

BEHOLD, THE ELEMENTS

The first snow comes like a thief in the night, a soft mantle of white blanketing slopes still streaked with golden aspen leaves. Heavy, damp, it bends the limbs of the evergreens, which droop like birds with their wings folded. It falls also on the geraniums and petunias in the planter boxes beneath the village windows, an undeniable reminder that the quietude of autumn is near an end, that winter and skiing soon will arrive. There is a new stirring, a quickening of the pulse in the village, a fresh urgency of preparation for the hurly-burly to come. Even in such a benign and premature form, snow starts working its magic on the mind.

But how can there be such sorcery in something no more complex than crystalline water, a substance which can be created by man with nothing more sophisticated than a nozzle spewing forth water mixed with compressed air? Yet skiers ascribe to it a divinity no less than the ancient Egyptians held for the life-giving waters of the Nile.

Indeed, the moisture has been delivered a comparable distance, boiling up in the Gulf of Alaska, rebounding off the peaks of the Wrangell and St. Elias ranges before hurtling south and east with all the fury inherent in a Pacific winter storm.

The tempest first strikes the coastal mountains—the Olympics and the Cascades, which siphon a lion's share of the moist bounty—then continues its journey across the continent. Depending upon size and direction, the storm next might visit the Sawtooth Mountains of central Idaho, a fresh thatch of powder for the slopes of Sun Valley. From there it could continue into the Madison Range of southwest Montana, where Big Sky resort awaits its own blessing of white, or to the Tetons and Jackson Hole, Wyo. If the path is farther south, the abundance falls on the Wasatch Range in Utah, where Snowbird, Park City and Alta exult in their reputation for bottomless powder.

Whatever is left comes to Colorado and, while there may be a bit less snow, there also is a decline in the wind and cold. Like the San Juans of southwestern Colorado, New Mexico's mountains take their snow chiefly from storms welling up off the coast of Southern California or Mexico or perhaps from a counter circulation of moist air from the Gulf of Mexico colliding with cold currents from the north. While the origins and routes of this snowfall is

Victorian facades recall Aspen's 19th century beginnings.

as diverse as the resorts it blesses, it all serves the same purpose—to make Rocky Mountain snow conditions the most consistent and dependable in all the hemisphere.

But snow would be nothing in itself without its marriage to mountains, a symbiosis which expedites the formation of the snow, the sculpting of the mountains, the creation of rivers, and the inspiration for some of our loftiest dreams. It should be little wonder that the mountains which so often have given rise to mysticisms and dieties in other societies should give birth to yet another religious form. Like ancient Greeks seeking divine guidance from Olympus, skiers view their mountains with a fervor which borders upon worship. Mountains become modern shrines which are praised through endless summer debate and revisited with the enthusiasm of pilgrims of Islam bound for Mecca. The quick, dashing young racers and instructors whose honeycomb skis serve as replacements for Mercury's winged feet are the chosen gods of skiing and are accorded fanfare and awe—and sometimes myth—which might have caused the poet Homer to pale. The mystery and lure of mountains is as difficult to explain as the age-old pull of the sea, a siren call which similarly defies logical explanation. It seems sufficiently simply to acknowledge the existence of something very special, very real, and as old as man himself.

Yet the mountains came eons earlier. That zone of violent upheaval which geographers have come to call the Rocky Mountains (as if all mountains did not have their foundations in rock) had its origins in a series of cataclysms dating back to the Mesozoic Era. By upthrust and erosion, glacial advances and recessions, these mountains have evolved as we see them today—the most dominant geographic feature on the continent.

The location and shape of the rock masses which resulted, coupled with prevailing weather patterns, have combined to provide the Rockies with conditions which approach the skiing ideal. Snow comes early and stays late, a factor of dependability upon which promotional campaigns can be launched and vacations can be planned many months ahead.

Mountains make weather, ranging from those idyllic, dreamy days which inspire picture postcards to conditions which are both awful and awesome, raging storms which blow the life from everything in their path. Such is the suddenness and fury of a mountain storm that it can swallow an unsuspecting skier and block his flight to safety. It is never to be trifled with. Man must be content to understand it as best he can, to gratefully accept its bounty and to be wary of its wrath.

Mountain weather is unpredictable at best, consistent only in its changeability. Abruptions in altitudes and wind currents produce effects which feed upon themselves to brew howling storms from what moments earlier was a sunny day. Temperatures may vary many degrees from sun to shade, and the mere passing of an innocent cloud can send the mercury plummeting. Conditions grow potentially more severe with elevation. An accepted gauge is that a gain of a thousand feet of elevation is equal to a journey 300 miles closer to the North Pole.

Snow almost always falls heaviest on the highest and largest mountain mass, often the result of orographic precipitation. This occurs when a prevailing wind (almost always westerly in the Rockies) pushes an air mass against a mountain or ridge, causing it to rise, cool, and condense. The result is a cloud cap which seems to hover for hours over a peak, but in reality is a swirling, constantly changing band of precipitation which abruptly lowers, warms, and evaporates, as it flows down the lee side.

These winds sweeping in from the west hold powerful sway over Rocky Mountain skiing. They sometimes blow all the fresh snow off the ski slopes and into the trees, where it is of little use. But the same wind may also funnel disproportionate quantities of snow into the basins and bowls so favored by skiers for whom deep powder snow is the *raison d'être*. By the quirk of a wind pattern or the tilt of a ridge a skier's paradise may be created.

Not just any mountain is suited for skiing. It must be situated to receive ample snow, yet with a variety of terrain, a necessity of economics if a ski area is to attract patrons of diverse abilities. Further, it must be accessible, not difficult to reach by modern transportation. Like the proverbial tree falling in a deserted forest, even the most beautiful rhapsody of mountain and snow is meaningless if no one is there to hear.

Those mountain resorts which best satisfy all these requisites are identified by their success, by a skier plebiscite taken every winter. To some degree, it is an election each ski area must continue to win to survive. By this enduring criterion, the leading resorts of the Rockies are not difficult to identify. It is not by chance, then, that most are located in Colorado. These are Aspen, Vail, Steamboat, Winter Park, Breckenridge, Keystone, Copper Mountain, and Crested Butte. Utah gives us the deep snow abundance of Snowbird, Park City, and Alta, while there is a single major jewel in the crowns of three other states. They are Sun Valley in Idaho, Jackson Hole in Wyoming, and Taos in New Mexico.

That these resorts have evolved ahead of the rest—in fact, that the Rockies have come into skiing prominence— is as much the result of promotional wizardry as of this conglomeration of natural wonder. It is true that the mountains of the Rockies are larger and more varied; that the combination of elevation and distance from the ocean makes the snow lighter and more enduring, more dependable; that the weather is less hostile than that of New England or the Alps. But what good would all this be if no one knew? Even the finest actor has a press agent. The selling of the Rockies began with Harriman's Sun Valley and a calculated plan to make it a winter wonderland for all those Hollywood stars. The glamor rubbed off not just on Sun Valley, but on all of skiing.

An even more enduring windfall came in 1960, when much of the nation discovered skiing through the magic of television at the 1960 Winter Olympics at Squaw Valley. And when a fledgeling resort called Vail suddenly popped up in the heart of Colorado's mountains a couple of years later, the spurt had begun in earnest. Vail quickly became the standard by which subsequent ski area development —and promotion—would be measured and imitated.

This glorious blend of mountains and snow, the curse of the pioneers, awaited the invasion of a nation's skiers.

Skijoring, an ancient Nordic combination of horseman and skier, is a popular attraction at the Steamboat Springs Winter Carnival.

A medieval lady attends her knight in this mural at Taos in New Mexico.

THE FACES OF SKIING

The flash of a racer speeding downhill. An early riser tossing a spray of powder snow like waves breaking against a seawall. Laughing children playing follow-the-leader through snow tunnels in the woods. A splash of color against a stark background of white. Hotshot mogul bashers bouncing through the bumps like marionettes dancing on the end of a string. Daredevils turning flips while judges attempt to evaluate the degree of their madness. Wine and cheese on a sunny slope. A jumper soaring hundreds of feet through the still, crisp air. A rhythmic gliding across a rolling meadow. All these things, seemingly so different, so omnifarious, share a common bond. All are done on skis. Skiers exult in an almost endless variety of sundry activities which, given the variables of weather, snow, and slope, almost never are the same.

How do we ski? Let us count the ways. There is recreational frolicking down groomed slopes, the go-at-your-own-pace choice of the multitudes who line up at the ticket windows and lifts to enjoy the luxury of a comfortable ride up the hill, a process to be repeated as long as stamina and daylight permit.

Among these are skiers of skill and verve who will be first in the chair on a morning after a fresh snow. These are the powder hounds, for whom a single, weightless descent through deep powder is worth days in the pack.

First tracks. The urge among skiers is as primordial as life itself, much as a bear is compelled to scratch his mark on a tree to lay claim to his domain. For the skier first down a trackless snowscape the declaration is much the same: for at least this fleeting moment, the whole mountain, this microcosm of the entire ski world, belongs to him.

The feeling of powder skiing is floating on air, of being buried beneath feathery billows only to emerge into the sunlight to gulp air and poise for another plunge. The experience is orgasmic, the stuff of dreams. If the snow crystals pile deep enough, as they often do in the Wasatch Mountains of Utah, skiers must use snorkels to breathe, disappearing beneath the snow in a ritual of burial and rebirth which transcends mere symbolism. The essence of powder skiing is a reincarnation of the spirit which liberates a part of us too seldom used.

There are those who claim that powder is the Zen of the ski sport, an act of doing and feeling—never thinking. If you must demean the experience with conscious thought, it is likely that you cannot do it at all. The sensations are many: falling free, floating, an eerie silence save the whisper of skis on snow, tiny rainbows flickering through swirling snow prisms, smoke rings in the corners of the mind. In their obsessive struggle to give perspective to something which has so much sameness, skiers grasp at adjectives for powder snow. Champagne powder. Ah, champagne. Light, sparkling, delicate, intoxicating.

For those who seek out the steep and deep, powder skiing becomes something of a religious experience, an intensely personal ritual to be shared only with intimate friends. Among these there grows a bond which approaches brotherhood, an elitism which elevates them high above the mere mortals who never have known the sight and feel of an unbroken expanse of powder snow. Some search the earth for powder—from the Alps to the Andes, from New England to New Zealand—on a quest for the perfect blend of mountains and snow, for the ultimate run. But most often they can find it all in the Rockies, mountains of dreams.

There is yet another ski form which rivals deep powder. The vernacular given it hints broadly at the type of activity: mogul mashing, jumping the bumps. For the expert mogul skiing is at once an act of necessity and joy. Combine the elements of steep terrain and numerous skiers. The result is moguls, those bumps caused when several skiers turn at the same place, carving and pushing snow into a mound. This slope then becomes a dual challenge of steepness laced with obstacle courses. It no longer is enough simply to descend the mountain; rather it must be done with strength and precision, a command performance which requires the skier to maneuver deftly among bumps which may reach a height of four or five feet on particularly steep and busy runs.

To hit such bumps head-on is almost like crashing into

Ice skating and bonfires are part of the nighttime sport at Elkhorn in Sun Valley, Idaho.

a wall. The proper descent is a serpentine path around the sides and through the troughs. Such skiing requires special techniques, highly stylized methods of surviving this acrobatic and demanding form of skiing. The French have given us *avalement,* which literally means "swallowing," a description of the motion of leg retraction needed to absorb the shock of the bumps. A marriage of this technique to the knack of choosing the most advantageous course transforms a seemingly impenetrable maze of snow into an immensely satisfying experience.

Expert skiers have become so infatuated with mogul skiing that an entirely new arm of the sport has evolved around it. Bump skiing has become an integral part of an activity variously called Freestyle or, in more basic terminology, Hot Dogging.

Then there is the aerial competition, the ultra-private realm of the sport's gymnasts. Beauty and danger are blended in the flips and twists these daredevils perform, each one courting the critical eye of the judges and, too often, a bed in the nearest hospital.

But one can no more ask a freestyler to forsake his flips than a bird not to fly. This urge to soar also sends skiers up in hang gliders, which ride the wind currents down from the mountain top, sailing free above pedestrian skiers bound to the snow. These, too, crash upon occasion with even more terminal results. Whatever the consequences, birds must continue to fly.

Another facet of freestyle is ballet, which resembles nothing so much as figure skating on skis. It is performed on smooth, gentle slopes, and the emphasis is on form rather than speed.

First snow on wildflowers is a sign of a new ski season.

Ski tourers pause near a weather-beaten ranch house in the region of Telluride, Colorado.

In sharp contrast to those who seek excitement in crowds and applause are the denizens of the back country, cross-country skiers, wilderness adventurers. While possessing a kindred spirit which causes them to bridle instinctively at the growing throngs at established areas, at what they derisively call the "yo-yo" dependence on lifts, these hardy souls take several shapes.

By far the fastest growing part of skiing is touring, which numbered only a few scattered participants fifteen years ago, solitary souls generally thought a bit daft. Why else would anyone choose to use his own propulsion to ski, to actually climb uphill when he could so easily ride a lift?

Perhaps the reasons are entertwined with the jogging craze, with the nation's awakening to the call for fitness. Indeed, cross-country often is described as running on skis, but there is more to it than that. One of the greater appeals is that one can proceed easily and comfortably at his own pace. The run becomes no more than the skiing equivalent of a pleasant stroll in the forest, a soft communion with nature during that most quiet time of the year, buoying the spirit.

Although the winter forest is quiet, it seldom is dull. For the practiced eye, it is teeming with life. An ermine, with only its beady black eyes and tip of tail to spoil a perfect camouflage, pops suddenly from the snow, glances quickly about, and plunges in again, somehow running swiftly beneath the snow as if it did not exist to appear many yards away.

Perhaps this efficient predator is following the snowshoe hare whose misshapen, elongated tracks lead off into a dense stand of spruce. Or maybe it seeks the pine squirrel, which scampers across the snow to take refuge in the nearest tree at one's approach. There it will feast on cones or, later in the season, upon the tender buds which the trees send out as a welcome to spring. We may not always see the squirrel, but its mast along the trail tells us it is nearby.

Larger animals, deer and elk, long since have discovered the advantage of following the trail packed by ski tourers. It is a thrill to know these forest giants have passed so close, for the outdoorsman to identify them by their tracks. On occasion one sees them, dark tan figures lurking at the edges of the timber, unhurried, unafraid if he does not approach too close. Somehow they know he wishes them no harm in this time of greatest stress.

Ski tours may last a few hours or several days, depending upon one's ability and inclination. Whatever the duration, there is a thread of escapism which permeates the fabric, the need to get away from the bustle of civilization, to seek the quiet of the winter woods.

Reflecting the increased popularity of touring, almost all major resorts have established touring centers which offer equipment rentals, lessons, and even maintained trails for those who wish them. The United States Forest Service has responded by designating many miles of trails which generally follow summer hiking routes or old mining roads.

Still there are those who must drink more deeply from the wilderness cup. In summer you may find them clinging precariously from steep mountain faces or running rapids in kayaks. There can be little doubt as to their winter haunts. You will find them climbing resolutely up snowy mountains, skis strapped to their backs, or, if the pitch is not too steep, skiing uphill with the aid of a specialized binding which grants the heel freedom for climbing yet clasps it firmly for downhill descents. These are the ski mountaineers, the modern Father Dyers whose secular mission it is to save their own souls from the shackles of the mundane. They claim to hunger after untracked powder, but most of what they seek is folded deeply inside the tapestry of solitude.

With the growing interest in these backwoods activities comes another concern, that of safety. These mountains—so enchanting, so compelling—have an equal propensity for danger. The storms which bring the benediction of snow can also grasp the unwary skier in the chilling grip of death. An even more formidable danger is that of avalanche, which strikes even on those cloudless, Elysian days when the enchantment of the moment blurs the vision of an unpracticed eye. Each year dozens of skiers are buried beneath snowslides. This is not cause to be frightened of mountains, merely to take proper caution.

Among skiing's most elite group, there is little room for circumspection. There are the racers, intense, hell-for-leather competitors for whom success is measured in equal parts abandon and discipline. The gauge often is in milli-seconds, and the difference between a gold medal and obscurity comes in the blink of an eye or the slightest tremor in the edge of a ski being carved through a control gate.

Speed. Racers get high on it—a form of drink they don't have to carry in a bottle, a spirit to be conjured up from that private nook of the mind where our innermost fantasies are stored. Speed is a time warp which blots out everything. Faster, ever faster, gravity draws carefully waxed skis over the snow, right to the ragged edge. The body performs marvelous feats of strength and balance; there is no time to plan or think, merely to act. Racing, too, is a Zen form.

The greater the speed, the daring, the more abundant the reward. When Franz Klammer dashed wildly down the Olympic downhill course at Innsbruck in 1976, the world rose involuntarily from its collective easy chair to stare in awe and wonder at the television screen. It was not just that the Austrian won the race; it was the incredible, almost indescribable way he did it: scrambling, bouncing, arms flailing wildly, always on the brink of disaster. For spectators who had never seen snow, skiing assumed a startling new dimension, and the quiet, unassuming son of a farmer almost instantly became a global hero. For the racer, the enemy is not speed, but fear. "I have never been afraid of an accident," said Klammer, whose one great dread is not of going too fast, but too slow.

Racers' triumphs and failures alike are heralded in the world press and often are the subjects of heated debates on national honor. These national teams annually spend millions in the unrelenting struggle for superiority. Much of the support comes from an industry which uses racers as models for their research and as glowing testimonials for product value.

Every skier loves the sensation of going fast, even the children. Especially the children. Lilliputians in caps pulled down over their noses who never get tired or cold, who ski endlessly and, to struggling adults around them, disgustingly well. Small bundles of rainbow color which pop in and out of the forest like bright elves, whooping, laughing. The skiers of today, tomorrow, every year.

A MOUNTAIN GALLERY

Abraham begat Isaac; and Isaac begat Jacob; and Jacob begat Judas and his bretheren; and Judas begat Phares and Zara of Thamar; and Phares begat Esrom; and Esrom begat Aram...and Matthan begat Jacob; and Jacob begat Joseph, the husband of Mary, of whom was born Jesus, who is called Christ. So all the generations from Abraham to David are fourteen generations, and from David until the carrying away into Babylon are fourteen generations and from the carrying away into Babylon unto Christ are fourteen generations. The Gospel According to Saint Matthew, Chapter 1.

Every eye is on the stage of the auditorium at the small school in Steamboat Springs, Colo., that winter day in 1932. Resplendent in his red, white, and blue warm-up uniform, ski jumper John Steele speaks eloquently and emotionally of his feeling of pride in being a member of his nation's Olympic team, his delight in representing his home town before the world. Far in the back of the room a young boy still in grade school, small for his age, leaps spontaneously to his feet and shouts, loud enough for those around him to hear, "I'm going to do that. I'm going to be in the Olympics."

In 1948, Gordon Wren, still smallish as a man, soared to fifth place in Olympic jumping, then returned to Steamboat as John Steele had done. And Wren begat the Werners—Skeeter and Buddy and Loris—and Marvin Crawford; and they begat Jim Barrows and Jere Elliott and all those still to come.

Carl Howelsen, Steamboat's Abraham, had been primogenitor of it all—not forty-two generations, but far more than at any other place in the nation.

It is only fitting that Crawford and Wren, who learned their skiing on the little hill in town named after the old Norwegian, should be the first managers of the new development on the big mountain they sometimes climbed to ski as boys. Now, almost two decades later, it has emerged among the giants of the Rockies with a network of eighteen lifts strung like spider webs across 3,600 vertical feet of terrain.

Steamboat has all the trappings of modern skiing: banks of condominiums, fine lodges, restaurants, night life. But there remains something else which cannot be created from mere glass and steel. There is a feeling which lingers, which prompts the grizzled rancher who still ranges his herefords across the lush, broad valley, to strap on his skis, pull his western hat down a little tighter over his brow, and ride up the mountain chatting easily with a systems analyst from Cleveland.

Wren and Crawford still live here. So do the Werners and Barrows and Elliott and all the rest who are still alive. Where else on earth would they want to go?

Spring sun at Mid-Vail, Colorado creates a festive mood, with wine served in the Spanish style.

EVERY FEW minutes a sleek aircraft touches down on the asphalt runway nestled at the bottom of the valley in defiance of the laws of nature, but not the Federal Aviation Authority.

Aspen claims more private jets land there each winter than at any other spa. Considering the climate of rivals such as Palm Springs and Las Vegas, it is certain that more women disembark wearing furs.

In many ways Aspen—its mountains, its people—is bigger than life. Some observers insist that the people here are real, sincere, not at all like the *noveau riche* who congregate each winter just across the range at Vail. But others claim that even those longtime residents whose bumper stickers proclaim, "Get Revenge, Ski Dallas," don't really mean it, that the money is the only thing which counts. Perhaps the tipoff is that the Aspen Skiing Corporation, which operates three of the four ski mountains, is owned by Twentieth Century Fox, which made the purchase with its profits from "Star Wars." Equal parts Hollywood and Fat City.

There is more to Aspen than this. Much more. The town, a quaint mixture of the new and the very old, has a charm blended with raw excitement which enchants even the most casual visitor. And the skiing. Ah, the breathtaking skiing. What most resorts dream of on one mountain Aspen has four times over.

The focal point, if for no reason other than location, is Aspen Mountain, also called Ajax. By itself it is one of the world's great mountains for experts. It is the mountain everyone says he skis, whether he really does or not. A favorite Aspen game, among many, is to take a late-afternoon ride up the short lift which serves the gentle lower slope. This allows the lesser skier the gambit of swooping down off the big mountain to rest his skis against the balcony of Little Nell's, gathering place of all the beautiful people, the place to see and be seen. Here skiers ogle each other and weave elaborate fabrications as to marital status and what mountain each skied that day.

Where most should have skied is Buttermilk, a full-scale mountain which would be an absolute prize in the East, but ranks merely as Aspen's teaching mountain. If it is at least partially true that Buttermilk is for the novice, then Snowmass is a towering monument to the intermediate. Its broad, gladed slopes are cruising country, a delight for skiers of all ability and the focal point of a self-contained resort community complete with elegant lodging and sumptuous dining.

The fourth member of the quartet is Aspen Highlands, independent in management and air. Highlands' vertical, 3,800 feet, is the longest in Colorado, and at a magic place near the top there unfolds one of the grander views in all of skiing. Hanging there in the distance like some giant, frosted Christmas tree ornaments is the twin massif of the Maroon Bells.

Singly, each of Aspen's mountains is impressive enough. Collectively, they must be skied to be believed.

* * * * *

JEAN-CLAUDE KILLY, the French Olympic hero whose conquests took him to the finest ski mountains around the globe, had but one answer when asked his favorite American resort. Even when he was being paid to represent a lesser area nearby, Killy could not lie. His choice remained Vail. Perhaps there was something with personal meaning, something which reminded him of his home in the French Alps. More likely, it was because Vail is the resort for the skier who has—or wants—everything.

It isn't enough that Vail is the largest single mountain skiing complex in North America with its ten miles of terrain, more than 700 acres of it in natural bowls, eighty-nine trails, runs four and one-half miles long. Or that there are sixteen chairlifts and a six-passenger gondola which transport more than 20,000 skiers each hour. Or that the sparkling, elegant village and the assortment of lodges which have sprouted up down the valley can provide pillow space for 22,000 visitors.

The image of Vail is of quality rather than quantity, of management concepts which set the tone for a score of others which came later. It can be argued convincingly that Vail is the most important ski resort ever built, both the role model and inspiration for a flurry of cloning which has made Rocky Mountain skiing what it is today.

The successors have chosen to refer to themselves either as "a Vail-type development" or "potentially as large as Vail" (none has made it) or, depending upon the degree

Skiers head for the slopes of Breckenridge on the west side of the Continental Divide in Colorado.

Colorado's Keystone ice arena has been the site of international skating events.

of snobbery forcibly impregnated into the project, "not at all like Vail."

Those who indulge in the latter view point to the "instant Switzerland" overtone of much of the village with the insinuation that the whole thing isn't quite real. Indeed, consternation swept the town on a recent Christmas when artificial evergreens were ordered to decorate the streets. The synthetics quickly went back into the box. There would be no holiday jibes of plasticity heaped upon the community.

If there is a judgement to be made, it is that Vail has been too successful, that the tidy little original village which Pete Seibert conceived and nurtured has leaped its bounds and spread like so much crabgrass. The Vail complex now extends for miles along the valley, an architectural hodgepodge which, if anything, is a testament to the immense appeal of the ski mountain.

That magnetism and, doubtlessly, the down-valley development will be heightened by the opening of a second Vail in December, 1980. The Beaver Creek project being completed by Vail's management just ten miles away is the most-anticipated, most publicized resort since, well, its sister area eighteen years before.

Planners say it will be as big and grand and successful as Vail, but all those other resorts have been saying the same thing, and it hasn't happened yet.

* * * * *

MUCH LIKE THE toes of a large bird, three valley prongs extend deep into the lofty mountain country of a central Colorado county called, appropriately, Summit. It was here that John Dyer, the Snowshoe Itinerant, skied among his flock more than a century before, and it perhaps was this rarified atmosphere which helped create one of the most rollicking mining districts in the entire West. Even discounting the imagination of a breed which, by profession, had to be nine-tenths dreamer, these old mining camps had a special ring: Montezuma, Chihuahua, Argentine, Kokomo, Humbug Hill.

These were the surroundings in which operators like Gassy Thompson, certainly a spiritual precursor to present-day real estate men, could thrive. Hired by investors in a

claim of unknown value to dig a test tunnel through 100 feet of solid rock, Gassy began to bore in earnest in the late fall beneath the watchful gaze of his employers. As winter storms began to sweep the country, the investors left the dilligent Thompson to his labor, promising to return in the spring.

Finding a tidy tunnel precisely as they ordered it, the owners cheerfully paid the industrious miner his wage. Not until the warmth of June began to melt the snow was the fraud discovered. Instead of laboriously picking away at unyielding granite, Gassy had carefully timbered the hundred feet out through the drifts. Gassy's ruse was surely an annoyance to his employers, but the retelling has great meaning for skiers whose predilection for such reliable snow has made the Summit area the fastest growing ski complex in the nation.

The memory of Gassy Thompson lives in a trail named in his honor at Keystone resort, but his spirit permeates the adjacent resorts of Breckenridge and Copper Mountain as well. Collectively, they comprise a marketing combine called Ski the Summit, which very soon could record more than two million skier days in a season—far more than the four areas of Aspen, far more than Vail.

Imagine, if you will, that each toe on this bird's foot is only fifteen miles apart, that the epicenter is but seventy-five miles from Denver, that they are connected by a free shuttle service, that there is an interchangeable lift ticket, and that each mountain and village offers its own separate charms. Now you understand the reasons for such high acclaim. There is something else: the kind of easy, cruising skiing which is like a magnet to tourists and family groups.

Oldest and largest is Breckenridge, which survived all those booms and busts of the mining era to redecorate its slab-sided, tin-roofed buildings in the best of mountain modern. Plush condominiums and ramshackle cabins share the upper Blue River Valley with the same ease with which it always has accommodated a similar diversity in its people. Focal point of it all is a ski complex which has grown from one mountain to two in keeping with the Summit surge. A network of lifts weaves like strands of a spider's web across the face of the Tenmile Range.

Several original 1880s buildings are still in use in the old gold mining town of Crested Butte, Colorado.

With few exceptions, Breckenridge is a pussycat of a mountain, the kind almost everyone can ski. But those exceptions are mentioned in hushed tones. Mach I, a plunge which looks from the top a lot like the view from the roof of a tall building, has an eighty percent gradient, steepest in Colorado. Nearby is another run with an equally descriptive name, High Anxiety, and terrain to match. In addition, there is a new chairlift to whisk skiers above timberline into broad powder bowls and open up additional terrain for the expert seeking exhilarating trails.

Keystone, named for the old stage stop and ore depot where Gassy Thompson made his getaway, is a testament to corporate efficiency and middle America's passion for comfort. The mountain and its sleek environs are a development of Ralston Purina. The guests are enthusiasts from Denver who fell in love from the start with this big, rolling mountain and well-heeled tourists from the same midlands which produce all the feed and grain for those checkerboard sacks.

It is not the kind of ski area sought out by the mogul-mashing fast guns of skiing. There are no trail names which suggest terror and imminent destruction. Rather, it is a rollercoaster of a mountain, the kind designed for invigoration instead of intimidation, the kind which makes you want to throw back your head and yodel, if only you knew how.

With the infusion of seemingly limitless Ralston capital, Keystone has grown to the spaciousness which one expects from a first-cabin Colorado resort, and the support facilities centered around a magnificent lodge may best be described as luxurious.

With the 1977 purchase of Arapahoe Basin, for more than three decades one of the skiing landmarks of the West, Keystone has added yet another feather in an already imposing headdress. Cradled beneath the ragged spires of the Continental Divide six miles to the east, Arapahoe provides a feeling of wilderness skiing without leaving the comfort of a triple chairlift. But all the vintage thrills remain: deep powder snow, steep chutes, the pervading presence of raw granite. However, with the coming of the Ralston corporate consciousness, there has been a kind of sprucing up, of comfort that Arapahoe regulars never dreamed of. The result has been to give Keystone the dimension of advanced skiing and high alpine excitement it needed to become a totally contained resort.

Copper Mountain never needed any such acquisition. From the start, its remarkable terrain has been clearly the best of the Summit trio, or quartet, depending upon how one measures the Keystone complex.

Copper likes to refer to itself simply as "The Mountain," a seemingly ostentation which is earned. When it was developed in the early 1970s, it was widely conceded that Copper was the finest untapped ski mountain in the state. Plainly, it also is superior to a great majority of its predecessors. Part of the reason comes in a unique geographic division of its slopes—expert on one side of the mountain, beginner on the other, and a broad band of intermediate trails in the middle. It is the kind of skier segregation, best for enjoyment and safety, that every resort seeks. At Copper, nature seems to take care of almost everything.

Certainly this is the case with the expert runs so scarce and valued among the Summit group. They start at timberline, just over the ridge from the aborted digs which produced only a low-grade copper ore, yet gave the mountain its name. And they continue all the way to the base, down

the gnarled snow fingers which form some of the most exciting advanced skiing in the region. Its steep rolls and ridges, all pocked with demanding moguls, are a delight to the skier looking for a challenge and all the reason the novice needs to retreat to the ease and comfort of the other side of the mountain.

The intermediate sits smugly in the center, perfectly positioned for a skier to nip over to either side and sample the best of each. These words—the best of it all—do much to describe the collective rewards which await skiers at Colorado's Summit.

* * * *

OF ALL THE trains which poke their blackened noses like some hyperactive worm through the West Portal of Moffat Tunnel, this one is special. Like all the others, it has negotiated the long, serpentine climb up the east slope of the Rockies from Denver to disappear inside the ten-mile-long bore beneath the Continental Divide. It isn't just that it runs only on weekends or that the cargo is so different or that it spends hours on a siding at the foot of one of the nation's most popular ski areas. Rather the Winter Park ski train is an institution, one which is as much a part of the ski sport as the mountain itself, both a reflection of the past and a hope for the future. For more than thirty years the train has disgorged its load of noisy, excited skiers, then, after the lifts close, carried them back through the tunnel and down to the city.

Young and old set their own pace in a Nordic cross-country race at Breckenridge, Colorado.

If the train is part of history, so too is the ski area, the result of a vision at a time when the notion of skiing was as foreign as gasoline shortages. At a time when few western cities gave much thought to outdoor recreation, Denver was busily acquiring a network of mountain parks designed as an escape from urban pressures. The one which opened in 1940 at the mouth of the tunnel was called, simply, Winter Park.

So apt a name has stuck with the place, even though a metamorphosis which has seen its way past so many layers of skin, so much growth. Once little more than the comfortable old shoe of a place where a city came to learn to ski, it still serves that function and more. The evolution

Handicapped skiers from across the nation take part in a special ski program at Winter Park, Colorado.

also has transformed Winter Park into a full-fledged resort with lodges and condominiums and all the other tourist trappings. It now ranks as the nation's largest ski area in close proximity to a major population center.

In fact, there is no longer just Winter Park, but two. The older complex, most of it gentle terrain, has been complemented by the steeper, more demanding chutes of the adjacent Mary Jane development, which may be the only ski area ever named after a prostitute. This historic name of the area was adopted from the prominent placer-mining claim at the base of the mountain. Legend has it that the claim was named for a particularly popular sporting woman who operated one of the region's most successful early enterprises.

There can be no doubt as to the present economic motivation of the valley. Like the trains which pour through the tunnel, Winter Park just keeps on rolling.

* * * *

IF EVER THERE was a shred of doubt that southerners—a smug lot who once took comfort in winter warmth while the rest of the nation shivered—have gone slightly bonkers over snow and cold and skiing, we give you Crested Butte.

The link is unmistakable. Southern ownership and a convenient location in the south central mountains of Colorado make Crested Butte a natural focal point of the station wagon route up out of Texas and points east. They haven't begun dispensing mint juleps in the cafeteria yet, but the soft, slow voice of the Southland always can be heard rippling across the snow on one of those frequent sunny, picture-perfect days at The Butte.

The Butte, as the locals abbreviate it, takes its name from the 12,171-foot peak with the majestic rock crest which holds the ski runs to its north-facing bosom much like a mother cradles a newborn. Most of these are gentle, ego-boosting trails precisely suited to skiers who see snow only a few days a year. But higher up in the shadow of the granite crest are a series of massive snow bowls designed to give a case of terminal knock-knees to the tyro who might dare venture there.

At least part of the charm of this wonderland of open snowfields and broad vistas is the dichotomy of the two towns which share it. The first is the relic of a mining town down in the valley, a survivor, a mixture of past and present where the residents alternately rail against becoming another Aspen and then do all the things to help make the transfiguration complete. Connected to the old town by a winding two-mile umbilical cord of a highway is the new town of Mt. Crested Butte, equal parts present and future. Its condos and lodges, most of them sparkling fresh and sprouting by the minute, surround the mountain like outposts around a castle.

An enduring debate, old vs. new, over the growth of tourism has been shelved to face a common foe. A proposed molybdenum mine, potentially one of the world's largest, threatens to reduce a nearby mountain landmark to rubble and slag and flood the valley with a wave of boom-town growth unmatched even at the peak of the gold rush. It is plain that Crested Butte's future remains with its mountains. But will it be high on the shining snowfields or deep within the pit of a mine?

* * * *

A JET TOUCHES down at the Salt Lake City airport, swings back down the runway and across the apron toward the terminal. On one side of the plane a score of noses press hard against the windows, gaping at what they have come halfway across the country to see.

Rising like a clerestory straight from the suburbs—so close it almost seems you can reach out and touch them—are the snow-thatched flanks of the Wasatch Mountains. America's powder bowl. Home of adventure. Heaven to the skier who prides himself in being able to turn 'em both ways.

There is a pioneering spirit alive in the Wasatch, a flame still flickering, perhaps, from the fervent fire of the Mormons whose wagon trains settled this second Promised Land. It is a place surging, pulsating with an urge to do and build and create at a time when other regions hotly debate the merits of more ski resorts or simply run out of feasible ski sites.

If the decades of the '60s and '70s ushered in the ascendancy of Colorado as the core of American skiing, then the '80s well could belong to Utah. This should not suggest that Utah has lagged in the past. More properly, it has been different, an observation which prompts a chorus of hallelujahs from the many devotees. Gentle slopes groomed as smooth as a baby's bottom, banks of towering condominiums, fancy restaurants, a rocking night life—all of those creations which draw the tourist hordes like flies to honey—never have been an overwhelming part of Utah's lure.

But now two forces are moving inexhorably to thrust it squarely into the mainstream. The spate of new development in these mountains is making a more generous allowance for the pedestrian tastes of the majority. Growth spurts at areas like Solitude, Sundance, and Brighton will attract more tourism, as will such potentially massive resorts as Heritage and Deer Valley. Having left his mark at Vail, Pete Seibert is in the midst of another major coup at a place called Snow Basin. Seibert doesn't have to be told what makes the cash register ring.

Happily, there also will be more demand for what Utah already has in such abundance. The overall growth of skiing has produced an increase in the numbers of advanced skiers. And wherever they gather, their dreams drift up into the Wasatch. By the very nature of the mountains—those soaring, plunging rock escarpments which mold and hold those marvelous deep-snow bowls—Utah skiing can never be called easy. More hallelujahs.

If the developing areas hold the keys to the future, contemporary success rests with Park City, Snowbird, and Alta—names which are magic to those who take their skiing straight from the hip.

Because it does have more intermediate skiing, Park City remains the most popular of the Big Three. Park is snow without the steep, a wide variety of defined runs in contrast to the stark, unfettered snowscapes of its neighbors. In short, it is the sort of friendly giant of a ski area you might find in, say, Colorado.

There is much to excite the better skier in Jupiter Bowl, 650 acres of steep, ungroomed powder, And there is plenty of life down at the base amid the Victorian gingerbread of the old mining town strung along a main street called, appropriately, Park Avenue. Like much of Utah's skiing, Park City is less than an hour's drive from the Salt Lake airport, and nearly half of the people who ski the major resorts stay in the city and avail themselves of the regular and inexpensive public transportation.

The love affair with the Wasatch has its heartbeat in a narrow, glacier-carved canyon cut like a blow from a giant cleaver straight into the center of the range. Little Cottonwood Canyon is steeped in history, mystery, and, sometimes, tragedy. That it has evolved as the epitome of the rugged, embrace-nature approach to skiing is totally in keeping with an equally raucous past. During the silver boom days just after the Civil War, more than 2,000 claims were filed in the canyon, many of them centered around a bawdy camp called Alta high in the massive snow basin at the head of the drainage.

Mining never was easy in a place sometimes blanketed by twenty feet of snow and rocked by avalanches which regularly ricochet down the narrow side canyons, burying everything before them. An 1874 slide destroyed half of the town and killed sixty people, and a single storm in 1965 dumped more than 10 feet of snow on the area. Clearly, this is the stuff of skiing legend, but sheer misery for the hearty souls clinging to a precarious existence after the bust.

For a time, only one prospector remained, a singular man named George Watson, who, in one of the most decisive ballots in the history of the democratic process, elected himself mayor. At some point in his many hours of snowbound contemplation, Mayor Watson concluded that his domain was probably better suited for the up-and-coming sport of skiing than useless chiseling on hard rock.

Watson enlisted the help of Alf Engen, then commuting from his ski teaching at Sun Valley, and together they gained support from businessmen in Salt Lake City. Watson donated 600 acres of land to the Forest Service expressly for the creation of a ski area, other mining concerns gave the rest, and the package was complete. In 1938 Alta ski area was born, and the nation's concept of the ultimate powder skiing experience was forever changed.

It was here by necessity that much of the avalanche research and control methods so routinely used now by all ski areas were developed. Even today, Alta remains something of a wild, untamed place. There are few frills: just five lodges, a few condominium units, and much the same

lift service that existed a decade ago. Alf Engen remains as director of the ski school after all these years, a septuagenarian still able to take almost any young hotshot up to the paralyzing plunge of High Rustler or into the Baldy Chutes and ski the stretch pants right off him.

There is another side of Alta, gentler and less publicized. It exists in a wide swath of intermediate terrain in Albion Basin, where lesser skiers can make their peace with powder over terrain which dictates only that they turn sometime, not where.

That Alta could remain so basic, so unprent0entious, is even more remarkable when compared to its chic new neighbor just one ridge and one road mile down the canyon. Snowbird was founded in 1971 by Texas Oilman Dick Bass as the posh, modern resort Utah never had. Upon rounding a bend in Little Cottonwood and seeing what appears to be a loose collection of concrete bunkers, one wonders what Bass and his associates had in mind. The structures are, indeed, concrete, left gray for an esthetic blend with the towering granite walls which surround them and decidedly reinforced to withstand the potential of heavy snow loads. But beneath this somewhat drab facade, Snowbird is as modern as they come. There are fine lodges, excellent restaurants, as much night life as Utah law allows, and the foundations for a ski operation which is as progressive as any in the country. The Snowbird company operates everything—lifts, ski school, lodges, food service—and the result is a pleasant orderliness and organization foreign to many resorts.

Flying up into the clouds on the 125-passenger tram, with the sweep of the Wasatch growing more panoramic with each second of ascent, is worth the trip to Snowbird in itself. When the tram finally comes to rest on a windswept ridge above timberline, one feels transported to another planet.

The people at Snowbird are fond of saying that the nicest thing about the place is Alta. And vice-versa. The two, which share an interchangeable lift ticket and regular shuttle bus service, are good for each other. Of the pair, Snowbird actually has the most difficult terrain and, for the super skier, the thought of having all the snow and chutes of both boggles the mind. There is much to jog the senses in Utah skiing. And more to come.

* * * *

IT HAS BEEN forty-odd years since Averell Harriman built Sun Valley as an extension of his railroad, and the inhabitants of that bizarre microcosm called show business no longer flock there to the exclusion of all else. That they sometimes find other places to ski is a commentary on the proliferation of the sport rather than the state of affairs at Sun. The Valley has changed over the years in about the same proportions as, say, Hollywood. Few would debate that the transition has been kinder to Sun Valley.

What has evolved here variously has been described as the perfect ski resort, the finest expert mountain in America, or just plain heaven. By any name, the massive monolith jutting up behind the little cowtown of Ketchum in the midst of the Sawtooth Range of central Idaho is an extraordinary piece of ski terrain.

Pioneers and stockmen called the mountain Old Baldy. It has grown no younger, but the "old" no longer applies or is used. Oh, the ice rink by the still-famous Sun Valley Lodge where Sonja Henie twirled in the movies is still there as are the rooms named after Eddie Duchin. Sun Valley never will outgrow its roots, even if it wanted to.

But there is a newness, an accelerated pulse about the place, which plainly is of the present. It begins on the mountain, 3,400 vertical feet of tingling excitement. There isn't a serious skier alive who doesn't fog his glasses from panting over the luscious slopes on his first trip up a Baldy lift.

The most distinctive element of Baldy's runs is that they never quit. The pitch is uniform, relentless. Seldom does it flatten to permit cruising, resting. For the skier whose ego will not accommodate a pause, a trip down Baldy is a marathon dance which is equal parts ecstasy and survival. Leg muscles on fire, skiers breathe a silent prayer of thanks that the straight, steep shots down the Warm Springs side of the mountain are not a yard longer, then eagerly pole into the lift line to do it all over again.

On the River Run side, a series of steep chutes have been carved through the trees in a diabolic attempt to drain whatever resources a skier might have left. The steepest is perhaps the most famous single trail in the nation. As the name suggests, Exhibition plunges straight below a popular chairlift where the resort could charge admission to watch the wipe-outs. Back in the Midwest, developers put chairlifts on hills no larger than a mogul on Exhibition.

High up top, past a restaurant and warming house called Lookout, are the spacious and treeless Bowl Runs, which gave Baldy its name. Some skiers spend a week in this grand ampitheater of snow, almost a mile wide and 1,800 vertical feet down, with absolutely no urge to go anyplace else. Satisfied they are enjoying the best.

There are ample trails groomed for the intermediate on Baldy and, for the beginners, a separate minimountain called Dollar, where the ski school dispenses the wisdom and courage required to venture up on Baldy before vacation time expires. The other side of Dollar is Elkhorn, with its own slopes and alternative village, one of three separate lodging complexes within a two-mile radius.

Sun Valley Village has been expanded by condominiums and sparkling new lodges. Condos surround Ketchum in sharp contrast to its rustic past. Sun Valley has changed, but if you peek outside the historic old lodge to the ice rink and close your eyes, you still can imagine Sonja Henie twirling there with a soft snow sifting down through the branches of the evergreens.

* * * *

FROM THE TIME the first paleface laid eyes on the big valley tucked away in the mountains of northwest Wyoming, it was apparent there was nothing of the commonplace about it. The mountains called Tetons, which rear up to dizzying spires off the western valley floor, fairly well took care of that by themselves.

Early on it was called Jackson's Hole for the mountain man who first explored it, but it wasn't until a couple of other trappers began to spread yarns about the area that people really began to take notice. When John Colter ventured north out of Jackson Hole and came back with tales of steaming geysers and bubbling caldrons, doubters termed it "Colter's Hell."

Jim Bridger also roamed this territory which one day would be incorporated into Yellowstone and Grand Teton national parks. Aware of the jibes directed at Colter, Old Gabe opted for some sport of his own. With tongue

Carpenter Gothic wood church was built in 1883 during the gold mining days of Crested Butte, Colorado.

squarely in cheek, he told of hooking trout in the cold rivers and cooking them in the streamside geysers as he pulled them in.

So, too, have the tales grown about the ski area opened in 1966 along the southern tip of the Tetons. It's hard to exaggerate a ski area whose 4,139 vertical feet is the longest in the nation and whose horizontal sweep is as big as all outdoors. But skiers caught up in the euphoria of a first—or tenth—visit to Jackson try anyway. Lord knows, they really try.

They rave of a seemingly endless series of bowls, chutes, gullies, and ridges carved from granite by glacial recession to form natural catch-basins for the dozens of feet of snow which fall each season. They tell of skiing a whole week and never crossing their own tracks, of skiing 150,000 vertical feet in that week.

They also speak of the ride up the sixty-three-passenger tram, which sweeps up over all those terrifying headwalls and cliffs, where the involuntary and often simultaneous sucking in of breath sounds like the escape valve on a steam engine. There is talk of a run seven and one-half miles long and about how defined trails at Jackson Hole exist only in the mind, how it is difficult to remember the precise route you took down the mountain only minutes before. And they are not stretching the truth.

* * * *

IT IS COLD in the upper Gallatin River Valley, and sunrise has not yet threaded its way through the jumble of mountains to the southeast. Small patches of early morning fog hang over ice-free riffles in the crystal clear stream which winds beside the road.

At this happy point of the mid-70s, travellers in Montana do not concern themselves with meaningful speed limits or gasoline shortages. My car surges powerfully over the flat, open stretches of the road north out of West Yellowstone. The reason for my haste is clear to me. There will be just enough time for a quick breakfast, a change into ski clothes, and a place among the first up the lift at Big Sky, Montana's recent entry into the ski resort sweepstakes. Eagerness comes with anticipation of the new and unexplored.

Farmhouses mark the long miles as one drives from Jackson Hole, Wyoming to Sun Valley, Idaho.

Tires strain in the turn off the main highway, and I begin the twisting climb up the side valley which caught the eye and imagination of the late Chet Huntley, the television newsman and native Montanan who provided the impetus for the development.

The light is growing now, and I can make out wisps of smoke from fine houses which outline what in summer is a golf course, now a ski touring center.

Suddenly, as if pulled by a magnet, my eyes leap upward at something glowing bright and pink. The sun's rays have fallen full upon the bald spire of Lone Mountain, casting a fuchsia tint to the expanse of snow above timberline. As Rocky Mountain peaks go, Lone Mountain is not particularly tall at 11,166 feet, but it gains stature in its isolation, a Fujiyama in a region where mountains normally are more gregarious.

Snuggled beneath this crest are the ski runs, a somewhat modest collection which suffer by comparison to their neighbors to the south. There is a massive snow bowl, a haven for powder freaks, in an imposing cirque beneath the crown of Lone Mountain, but the skiing ranks as only good overall, not great.

Still, there is something about Big Sky. Perhaps it is in the absence of crowding, of clutter, in a setting of carefully contained beauty. It is a place worth driving a little faster to reach.

* * * *

SETTLE BACK FOR a moment, close your eyes, and let your fancy roam to a place of wild contrasts. It is a place where fresh snow sits like marshmallow frosting atop cactus plants a brief distance from a village so alpine in character that it must have been transplanted straight from Switzerland. This is New Mexico, where desert and mountain coexist in curious proximity, where there is skiing at roughly the same latitude as Montgomery, Alabama.

Here, the state's second largest ski area, Sierra Blanca, is owned and operated by the Mescalero Apaches, an enterprising tribe which also maintains a thriving summer resort business. Not to be outdone, the Rio Costillo Cooperative Livestock Association is making plans for a 2,000-acre ski complex near Taos, which could cost a conservative $100 million. So much for the old stereotypes about cowboys and Indians.

At Albuquerque, the capital, a tramway sweeps skiers right from the edge of the city up to Sandia Peak, where they frolic in full view of the skyscrapers below.

It is a testament to the success of the Mescaleros that Sierra Blanca thrives only a hundred miles north of Mexico, exceeded in size only by Taos Ski Valley, a little bit of Switzerland in the Rockies. That it comes off as real is because it was founded twenty-five years ago and built piece by painstaking piece by real, live Swiss. Ernie Blake doesn't plan for his resort to get much bigger, which probably still will keep it ahead of its neighbors.

In New Mexico skiing, sheer size seems to count for little among either area operators or visitors, most of them Texans who like the low-key, family-style atmosphere of the small ski towns and the equally hospitable mountains. An exception is Taos, tucked away in a lofty and wild mountain country just eighteen miles from one of the oldest Indian pueblos in the Southwest, itself a major tourist attraction.

The Sangre de Cristo Mountains, which form New Mexico's sharp spine and are host to its skiing, were named by some anonymous Spanish explorer. Equally devout and quixotic, he saw the setting sun cast its crimson glow on the high peaks and immediately thought of the blood of Jesus Christ.

Whatever real blood there may be there nowadays comes through the pores of less skilled skiers trying to negotiate the rugged trails which comprise much of Taos. A prominent sign at the entrance tells the story well enough and reflects Blake's straightforward humor: "Don't Panic! You Only See One-Third of Taos Ski Valley. We Have Lots of Easy Trails, Too."

Story has it that before Blake erected the sign, a succession of station wagons bearing Texas plates pulled into the parking lot, rolled down the window, took one look at the intimidating steepness and barn-size moguls on Al's Run, and kept right on going.

There is fine intermediate skiing in Kachina Basin, an interlocking addition just up the valley and, overall, a heady blend of snow and warm sunshine unmatched at any other North American resort—just another of New Mexico's contrasts which seem to sweeten the nectar.

The ski train has transported generations of skiers from Denver to Winter Park.

APOCALYPSE—

There is nothing quite so difficult to predict as the future, particularly if that future is entwined in the vicissitudes of the economy, energy supplies, and public land still available for use.

So it is with skiing, whose lift lines and ticket prices continue to grow while the numbers of ski areas do not, where the largest and most crowded become larger and more crowded. As with any activity which mixes the volatile ingredients of high profile, rapid growth, and massive investment, skiing becomes a prism which can reflect any number of shapes and colors. Everything depends upon the position of the observer.

When the U. S. Forest Service designates a mountain for ski development, cries of outrage are heard from those who want it for wilderness. Conversely, protests, delays, and drawn-out government studies cost developers millions and add to the soaring cost of lift tickets and the crowding of existing areas. At best, building a ski area is a costly and trying proposition. One ski developer once made a list of more than sixty political entities with whom he had to deal in his efforts to create a major resort. Several years and many millions later, he gave up and went on to other pursuits.

Even before the first shovel of earth was turned, Vail Associates spent $6.5 million on its Beaver Creek adjunct. Opening was planned for 1976, but delays relating to government regulations extended that by four full years. Against such uncertainty, development money is becoming increasingly difficult and costly to obtain.

Yet even the most avid skiers are concerned with the cluttered sprawl which threatens to create mountain versions of strip city in the narrow valleys connecting some resorts. Even among winter recreationalists, the cry for more ski areas is not universal.

Against the backdrop of such complexities, the sport finds itself preoccupied with a confusing alphabet game. We might call it the "Three L's" of skiing—litigation, legislation, and limitation.

There was a time when attorneys came to ski areas only to ski. Now, with a spate of suits involving skiers injured in falls, legal maneuvering has become as much a part of resort life as shoveling snow. Massive judgements and settlements threatened to drive liability carriers away from the ski market at a time when ski operators scarcely could afford to write their own. Mushrooming insurance costs are directly reflected in the spiral which has brought us nose-to-nose with a lift ticket which costs $20.

The legislation has come from all sides, much of it by opportunistic politicians who suddenly discovered the highly visible forum skiing presented every time it decided to poke its collective head up out of the snow.

There is growing concern that the new makers and shakers of the ski world seem to be lawyers and accountants, corporate to the core, obsessed with factoring out the profit potential of each snowflake as it drifts innocently toward earth.

Almost gone are the carefree pioneers who built ski areas as places they and their friends could ski. Taking their places are giant corporations whose emotional highs are recorded in black ink rather than in the sensation of weightlessness in deep powder.

In a trend suggestive of falling dominos, these corporations are moving toward multiple ownership of resorts.

Twentieth Century Fox operates three of the four mountains at Aspen, all of Breckenridge, and openly covets more. Brothers Harry and Richard Bass, their common economic roots in Texas oil, own Vail and Snowbird, respectively. Ralston Purina has both Keystone and Arapahoe Basin. Big Sky's parent company also controls a string of Michigan resorts. The beat goes on.

This infusion of clout might be expected to alleviate the lift-line pinch, but capacity continues to lag behind demand at many critical junctures of a season. An almost inevitable result has been the third "L." Limiting the numbers of skiers through ticket sales is a recognition of the finite capacity of the mountain, just as in a sports arena or a concert hall. While few could debate the need to protect the quality of the ski experience, there is widespread suspicion of how the tickets will be distributed. Will they go chiefly to tourists ensconced at the area? Can day skiers obtain their fair share? Equity may be a quicksilver glimmer in the eye of a dreamer.

The total irony of these tangled issues is that all may be decided at the gasoline pump. The uncertainty of fuel supplies hangs like a millstone around the necks of skiers and operators alike. There is small hope that ski travel will be given high priority in event of severe national shortages, and even smaller provision has been made for public mass transportation to fill the void. The Winter Park ski train may someday have a significance no one could have dared dream.

It perhaps is a testament to the raw appeal of skiing, the sheer exhiliration of it all, that there presently exist hardly any pessimists in the sport. Whatever trace there may be of doubt quickly dissipates on those magic mornings when bright sunshine twinkles and dances on fresh snow, when brightly colored gaggles of skiers storm the lifts, laughing and shouting all the while.

One wonders what Father John Dyer might think if he happened upon all this, looking down from some high, wind-swept ridge under the dual burden of his mail pouches and the doomed souls of a raucous flock basically beyond redemption. The old Snowshoe Itinerant might shake his head in wonderment at what he had begun so many years ago, then trudge off into the back country on those long, clumsy skis.

I'm not certain he'd understand.

Winter's contrasts are framed by a Park City fence.

31

Survivors in the eternal battle of mountain winter, weather-worn trees face yet another storm near the summit of Snowbird in Utah.

In the cold, clear atmosphere over the Rockies snow crystallizes into an airy powder that stays light and dry. Here, a skier at Snowmass in Colorado sends up a powdery cloud.

The slopes of 11,166-foot high Lone Mountain at Big Sky in Montana provide skiers with powder snow that is light, dry and deep.

Framed by a nice sign, the town of Telluride becomes a living postcard.
Proud residents proclaim it, "the most beautiful spot on earth."

*Cold, crisp nights of autumn change the leaves of aspen creating a
mosaic of gold among the evergreens on mountain sides near Vail, Colorado.*
Right: *First snow on changing aspen signals the beginning of a
new ski season.*

Skiers have been competing on Howelsen Hill at Steamboat Springs, Colorado, for almost six decades. Left: A ski patrolman is dwarfed by the immense snow bowls at Big Sky, Montana. Overleaf: The slopes at Steamboat are an open invitation to glorious skiing.

Vail, Colorado, the nation's single largest mountain ski area, comes alive in the still mountain air of early morning. Left: Vail's LionsHead gondola soars up almost 3,000 vertical feet, offering breathtaking views of Colorado's mountain peaks both winter and summer.

The deep snow so treasured by skiers can sometimes pile up creating a challenge of getting in and out for Crested Butte residents.

A ski tourer makes a detour on his cross country travels at Park City.

*A high-ridge skier samples Aspen Highlands, a giant mountain whose 3,800-foot
vertical is the longest in Colorado, but is only one of four mountains
in the Aspen complex.*

*Vast treeless snowscapes attract skiers high above timberline near imposing
Crested Butte.*

The bounty of Utah snow long has lured powder hounds from across the continent. Snow Basin, one of the state's several emerging resorts, gets more than its share.

Holly leaves are a reminder that not all visual splendors of skiing are in the dash of downhill runs or the flash of colorful outfits.

Balloons at Steamboat Springs loft intrepid skiers into the backcountry and fresh powder, a relatively new method that provides access and fun. Right: Glistening crystal in this Aspen shop matches the sparkle of the snow outside.

In Park City's gondola skiers soar on a breathtaking 23-minute ride above exciting terrain while winter snow decorates the bare limbs of an aspen. Left: An explosive flight through deep powder is one of the thrills of skiing the Rockies.

Part of the pleasure of skiing is in getting there, especially if you travel along the Yampa River on the road from Vail to Steamboat.

When spring is in the air—and on the snow—as in this high meadow near Crested Butte, it evokes a special verve in ski tourers. Overleaf: Citizen races, open to all regardless of skill, have become exciting events in the Rockies. Here, entrants in Colorado's Frisco Gold Rush sprint across the frozen surface of Lake Dillon.

The rugged crest and jagged peaks of Ten Mile Range tower between the Colorado resorts of Breckenridge and Copper Mountain. Right: Pushed by a storm, a lone skier breaks powder on Lone Mountain at Big Sky.

An off-trail skier tempts fate on the precipitous terrain between Snowbird and Alta in Utah. **Left:** *The back bowls of Vail are famous for their powder. Trailing clouds of snow, Tom LeRoy runs Milt's Face in Sunup Bowl.*

*For thrills, adventure—and danger—create your own trails on the
untracked expanse between Alta and Snowbird in Utah.*

Skiers who dare the Milk Run or the Plunge at Telluride in Colorado can appreciate the early prospectors calling the town "To Hell You Ride."

Like the Alps, the Rockies offer vast snowfields above tree line, giving the skier room to wander where the spirit leads.

*A multitude of lifts at Utah's Park City give skiers easy access to a variety of
slopes from steep runs for experts to broad comfortable glides for beginners.*

In sharp contrast to the narrow runs of the East, wide-open spaces are the hallmark of the Rockies. It's easy to lose oneself in West Basin at Taos in New Mexico.

First tracks—being first down a stretch of unbroken snow—brings a special joy to the skier at Keystone.

A cross-country skier executes a freestyle maneuver on Vail's Pima Run.
Right: Professional skiers in head-to-head competition create spine-tingling
excitement and drama, and vie for thousands of dollars in prize money.

Skiing the Mary Jane complex at Winter Park calls for both courage and skill.
Left: This narrow ledge leads to The Cornice at Taos. Overleaf: 11,750-foot
Mt. Timpanogos looms over the ski slopes of Sundance, Utah.

The beauty of winter goes far beyond the mere physical act of skiing. Some places, like this secluded spot near Aspen, are just for looking.
Right: Rising above it all at Steamboat.

74

The smile says it all about snow conditions at Snowbird. Left: U. S. Ski Team racer Andy Mill takes the high road on a downhill training run for the national championships at Copper Mountain.

*The varied, sometimes violent, moods of steep-walled Little Cottonwood
Canyon dominate the drive to Snowbird and Alta in Utah.*

*Aspen's carefully-maintained Victorian architecture stands in tribute to its past
and to the thoughtful people, such as Mr. and Mrs. Walter Paepcke,
who enriched and rejuvenated the community.*

*Plunging into space off Snowbird's Wilbere Ridge challenges both the skill
and courage of the super-expert skier.*

On occasion winter storms will close in on a skier, reducing visibility and providing more powder than is wanted at the moment such as here at Arapahoe Basin.

In freestyle competition, the event is called ballet, *which is appropriate for the grace champion Marion Post brings this stylized sport.*

The stimulating environment at Big Sky prompts a cross-country skier to try almost anything—even a telemark turn off a cornice.

A snowshoe rabbit, whose ability to traverse deep snow rivals that of skiers, left these tracks near Copper Mountain. Right: Freestyle pacesetter Wayne Wong skis on the wild side in Jupiter Bowl near the summit of Park City.

Prior to the race, professional skiers concentrate on memorizing each turn and gate—thinking their way down the course. Left: On the way down, the cry is universal—more speed. Overleaf: Spire Ridge in Utah's Wasatch Mountains provide dramatic background for daredevil run.

*Mt. Elbert, left, Colorado's highest at 14,431 feet elevation, and 14,418-feet
Mt. Massive dominate the high country around Leadville, where pioneers
once travelled on 12-foot skis.*

Jackson Hole, Wyoming offers slopes where skiers can descend over 4,000 feet and an aerial tram that takes just 12 minutes to return them to the top.

Floating on a cloud of powder in an almost ethereal world, Corky Fowler enjoys sublime skiing at Snowbird.

*A mogul skiing contest on Sun Valley's Exhibition slope demands the utmost
skill in maneuvering the treacherous mounds.*

Down, but laughing. Sometimes it can be as much fun under the powder as on it. Right: A lunchtime crowd on the deck at Mid-Vail enjoys munching with a view of fellow skiers and the forested slopes of the Gore Range.

*For the most part, skiing is an individual sport, but there are times a friend
makes it better, as when mogul hopping at Winter Park. Left: They call this
Sun Valley adjunct Dollar Mountain, but plainly it is worth much, much more.*

Children seem to have a magnetic attraction for snow, whether on skis or off.
Right: At Telluride, skiers take it slow and easy. Butch Cassidy was traveling
considerably faster after he robbed the Telluride Bank of $30,000 in 1889.

Taos, the crown jewel of New Mexico skiing, is an unusual blend of
Switzerland, cowboys, Indians, sunshine and, of course, deep snow.
Left: *Alta's High Rustler run, watched over by Superior Mountain.*

Signaling the first stirrings of the day, light from a bakery spills across a snow lawn at Telluride.

Coffee Pot Pass leads cross-country skiers through the solitary terrain between Crested Butte and Aspen. Overleaf: Patterned after the Vasaloppet in Sweden, Colorado's Frisco Gold Rush is a race in which everyone is a winner.

The Inn at Sun Valley is a landmark in skiing history, as part of America's first major Alpine ski resort. Right: Timber-bashing—when a skier doesn't find quite enough room between trees on the Shadows run at Steamboat.

Deep winter snow spells fun for skiers, but hardship for animals like these
mule deer picking their way across a Colorado hillside. Left: Skiing takes wing
on the slopes at 12,441-foot Copper Mountain, whose chairlift offers majestic
views of the Continental Divide and the Ten Mile Mountain Range.

The Tetons from the west, a view summer tourists seldom see, is a special reward for skiers who have discovered the Wyoming resort of Grand Targhee.

*On the super-expert Baldy Chutes at Alta, danger is your companion,
one slip and you get to kiss a rock.*

*Soaring steeple with its clock and rooster is a familiar landmark in
Sun Valley, a favorite resort of the nation's skiers.*

Snow ghosts—evergreens under crystal blankets of snow—sparkle under the bright sun at Grand Targhee, Wyoming.

Indians in the Taos area attached spiritual significance to Kachina Peak
in the background, skiers find the timberline skiing a no
less moving experience.

*The chutes above West Basin dwarf a lone skier, creating a dramatic sense
of the vastness of the ski realm at Taos.*

*The dawn patrol explores the expert terrain of Red's Run
on Aspen Mountain.*

*A famous silver mining camp since the 1870s, Park City maintains its
sturdy mine building as part of its rich history.*

*No quarter is asked and none given for the expert skiers who seek
out the steep and deep at Snowbird.*

Exhilarated skiers claim a descent on the Crested Butte face known
as The Nose is almost the equivalent of free fall. Overleaf: At Snowbird,
a popular sport is racing downhill in an attempt to beat the tram.

Hang gliding is a sport practiced over land and sea, but enthusiasts at Aspen Highlands say it is best over snow, where the bonus is a swift in-run on skis.

Skiing might be termed an equal opportunity sport; the skier bursting through a wall of loose snow at Copper Mountain has an even chance of making it.

Despite the ample snow harvest of the Rockies, it sometimes helps to give mother nature a hand.
Snow guns, like this one on Vail's Golden Peak, help to improve conditions on
lower slopes and extend the season each year.

Safe passage through a thicket of slalom poles is the goal of a Copper Mountain racer. At the international level, racing demands training and discipline exceeded by no other sport.

Snow-encrusted thistle blossom surrenders a final sip of pollen, prelude to a new winter. Right: At Vail, "going to China," is a popular journey to China Bowl for the celestial delight of Alpine or cross-country skiing.

PHOTOGRAPHING SNOWY THINGS

The reflective quality of snow and how it affects my photography in the mountains during the winter has always fascinated me. It is a technical problem that I have mastered over the years, but it is always interesting to see how it affects the things I photograph.

When trying to explain this phenomenon of reflective light to a magazine publisher, I resorted to theatrical gestures. After watching me for a while, he finally leaned back and said, "Yeh, Barthel, you mean the snow *irradiates*." "Thanks, Brett," I mumbled and went to Webster's. While consulting the dictionary, I discovered his word did describe precisely what I wanted to say, and more! "Irradiate—to illuminate, to brighten." Exactly. Every object surrounded by snow actually is illuminated twice—once by the sun and once by the reflection of the sun off the snow.

With proper metering on a clear day everything is fine for there are usually only one or two camera settings required all day. (One for front light and one for back light.) On a stormy day, however, the light is constantly changing due to the varying density of the cloud layers. The snow continues to irradiate subjects on the slopes, so the need to change settings increases up to four or five settings every *minute* while storms roll in. Add to that the difficulty of skiing in storms where visibility, wind, and cold hamper all efforts to photograph. Before I learned to understand and use that light, I would rather spend those storm days in my studio shooting fashion models.

Now I use that changing light to advantage. It has resulted in producing some of my most successful photographs. With the challenge comes the reward. Learn to study the light, and use it effectively while it changes.

By leaving the studio and working in the outdoors, I have enjoyed a second definition of the word irradiate . . . "To enlighten intellectually or spiritually." I have spent the last 20 years in the mountains and in doing so have experienced both spiritual and intellectual enlightenment. Standing on top of mountain ranges in the Rockies or the Alps as the sun sets, watching the light play off the snow and back against the clouds . . . to see a storm drift across the desert and wrap itself around the Wasatch Range in Utah . . . these mind pictures I have forever. I feel big and then again I feel small. It is really something for poets to write about.

Finally, (believe it or not) irradiate also means . . . "to treat with some form of radiant energy, such as ultraviolet light." These invisible rays lie in the part of the spectrum beyond violet, and while invisible to the human eye, they are recorded by photography. They are one of the crummy things photographers at high altitudes must deal with. Atmospheric layers and air pollution block them out at lower elevations and produce beautiful warm oranges, pinks, and reds at sunset. Glowing skies with purple painted clouds . . . just made for lovers. But there is no air pollution in the high altitudes of the Rockies and the ultraviolet light is recorded. It unbalances conventional, professional film with hues of blue . . . something not made for lovers or photographers. Although film could be made to compensate for ultraviolet light, film manufacturers *won't* deal with it so the photographer must properly filter it out. So this is the only tip I have for those people who care to schlep their cameras up the ski slopes: follow the instructions that come with your film, use an ultraviolet filter, and just as important, take your favorite bottle of wine.

Irradiate—a word that means so much to photographing the ski scene in the winter Rockies.